DRAW ME HEALTHY

A STICKY BOOK

WRITTEN AND ILLUSTRATED BY BRANDON REESE

Review&Herald®
REVIEW AND HERALD PUBLISHING ASSOCIATION
SINCE 1861 | WWW.REVIEWANDHERALD.COM

Published by Review and Herald® Publishing Association, Hagerstown, MD 21741-1119

Review and Herald® titles may be purchased in bulk for educational, business, fund-raising, or sales promotional use. For information, e-mail SpecialMarkets@reviewandherald.com.

The Review and Herald® Publishing Association publishes biblically based materials for spiritual, physical, and mental growth and Christian discipleship.

This book was
Edited by Jeannette R. Johnson
Designed by Brandon Reese
Cover art by Brandon Reese
Typeset: Jason Text 14/16.8

PRINTED IN U.S.A.

17 16 15 14 13 2 3 4 5

Library of Congress Cataloging-in-Publication Data
Reese, Brandon.
Draw me healthy! : a sticky book / written and illustrated by Brandon Reese.
p. cm.
1. Health—Juvenile literature. 2. Nutrition—Juvenile literature. 3. Exercise—Juvenile literature. I. Title.
RA777.R43 2013
613.2—dc23
2012024023

ISBN 978-0-8280-2680-2

To Ann, my mother . . .

who provided me with blank pieces of paper
to draw on and a strong foundation to draw from.

Before you get started, you will need three things:

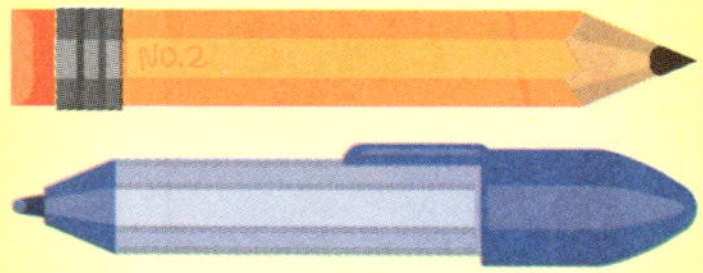

a pencil or pen

a pad of standard
yellow sticky notes

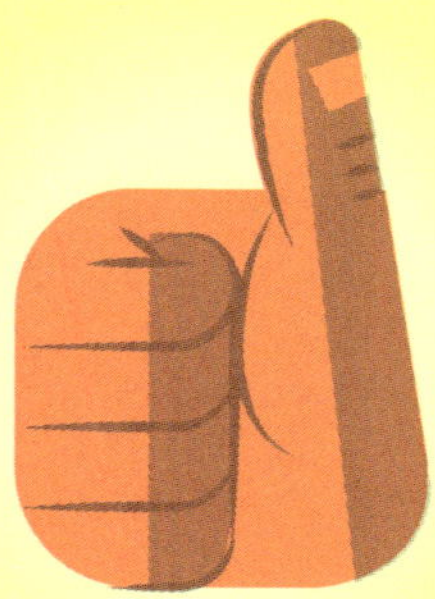

and, most important,
you like to draw fun stuff!

When you see a dotted box, place a sticky note there and follow the directions.

Turn the page, and let's draw!

Did you know that God wants us
to live a healthy and happy life?

There are eight simple ways to help us do that,
and there's a neat way to remember them.

Just think NEW START.

Draw what you think a girl's happy and healthy face looks like.

Draw what you think a boy's happy and healthy face looks like.

This is Noah. Does it look as if he is living a healthy and happy life?

Let's help Noah. Get Noah's attention!

Draw something that will get Noah's attention: an alarm clock, a barking dog, an air horn—something to get him up and moving!

Draw a bucket of
cold water to
splash on Noah.

That didn't work. Noah still won't move. I'm sorry it's come to this, but I think we need to splash Noah with a bucket of cold water.

Yikes! I can't believe
you did that!
I'm up; I'm up!
Please give me something
to dry off with!

Draw a towel or hair dryer—
something to dry Noah with.

Draw Noah’s messy hair.

Uh-oh . . . Look at my hair!
I can't go out like this.

Draw a brush or comb.

I think I'm ready for my
NEW START.

Draw something healthy
for Noah to eat.

N is for NUTRITION.

Nutrition is the food you eat. Healthy food gives you energy. We need energy to make our muscles move and help our brains to think.

E is for EXERCISE.

Exercise is anything that gets your body moving and your heart pumping. Noah would like to jump rope.

Thanks for the yummy food.
It gave me a lot of energy!

Draw a rope
for Noah to use.

. . . 98, 99, 100 . . .
Whew! What a workout!
I sure am thirsty.
You know what would be great?
Some cold water.

Draw Noah some water in a fancy cup or glass.

W is for WATER.

Drinking several glasses of water every day helps our bodies flush out all the bad stuff.
It's refreshing, too!

Draw a bright, shining sun.

S is for SUN.

It's good to get at least 10 minutes of sunshine a day. But don't stay in the sun too long. You don't want a sunburn. Ouch!

Ah, that sunshine feels good on my skin.
SPF 30

Draw a mean cloud.

T is for TEMPERANCE.

Temperance is staying away from things that are harmful to our bodies, such as smoking cigarettes or drinking alcohol.

Ugh! I need to get away from that nasty smoke. Can you draw a mountain for me to climb? I need to breathe some fresh air.

Draw a mountain
for Noah to climb.

A is for fresh AIR.

Breathing fresh air helps you to think better and gives you more energy.

Whew! Why did you draw such a big mountain for me to climb? I'm tired and need some rest.
Will you draw a pillow for me to rest my head on?
Draw a comfy pillow.

R is for REST.

It's best to get eight to 10 hours of sleep each night.

T is for TRUST IN GOD.

God likes us to talk to and trust in Him.

Draw something you
would like to pray for.

Now that you have learned about your NEW START, try the healthy workout below!

The burpee—funny name, but a great full-body workout. No equipment necessary!

Step 1: Start at standing position.

Step 2: Squat down. Plant your hands on the ground in front of you. Kick your legs back into a push-up position.

Step 3: If you can do a push-up, do one. If not, go on to step 4.

Step 4: Hop to your feet, bringing your feet back under you into the squat position.

Step 5: Rise to standing position, jump in the air, and clap your hands above your head.